THIS WHERE'S WALLY? BOOK BELONGS TO:

_____

_____

HEY, WALLY FANS! FIVE INTREPID TRAVELLERS ARE LOST IN EVERY SCENE! CAN YOU FIND THEM?

ODLAW   WIZARD WHITEBEARD   WENDA   WOOF   WALLY

AND IN EVERY SCENE, THE TRAVELLERS HAVE EACH LOST SOMETHING PRECIOUS! CAN YOU FIND THEM TOO?

WALLY'S KEY   WOOF'S BONE   WENDA'S CAMERA

WIZARD WHITEBEARD'S SCROLL   ODLAW'S BINOCULARS

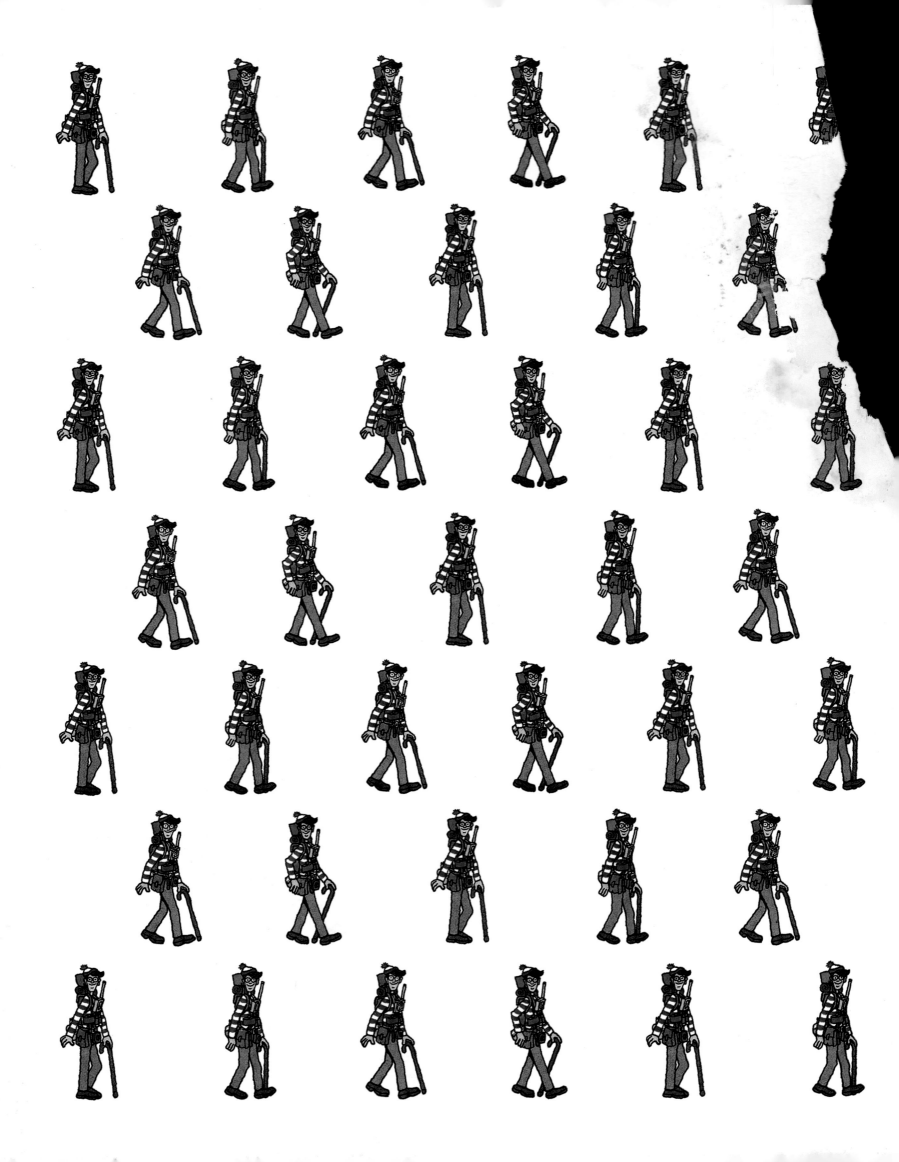

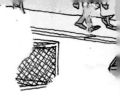

For Wally

First published 1987 by Walker Books Ltd
87 Vauxhall Walk, London SE11 5HJ

This edition published 2015

2 4 6 8 10 9 7 5 3

© 1987 – 2015 Martin Handford

The right of Martin Handford to be identified as author/illustrator
of this work has been asserted by him in accordance with the
Copyright, Designs and Patents Act 1988.

This book has been typeset in Wallyfont and Optima.

Printed in China

British Library Cataloguing in Publication Data:
a catalogue record for this book
is available from the British Library.

ISBN 978-1-4063-6117-9

www.walker.co.uk

WHERE'S WALLY?

MARTIN HANDFORD

WALKER BOOKS

AND SUBSIDIARIES

LONDON · BOSTON · SYDNEY · AUCKLAND

HI FRIENDS!

MY NAME IS WALLY. I'M JUST SETTING OFF ON A WORLD-WIDE HIKE. YOU CAN COME TOO. ALL YOU HAVE TO DO IS FIND ME.

I'VE GOT ALL I NEED — WALKING STICK, KETTLE, MALLET, CUP, RUCKSACK, SLEEPING BAG, BINOCULARS, CAMERA, SNORKEL, BELT, BAG AND SHOVEL.

BY THE WAY, I'M NOT TRAVELLING ON MY OWN. WHEREVER I GO, THERE ARE LOTS OF OTHER CHARACTERS FOR YOU TO SPOT. FIRST FIND WOOF (BUT ALL YOU CAN SEE IS HIS TAIL), WENDA, WIZARD WHITEBEARD AND ODLAW. THERE ARE ALSO 25 WALLY-WATCHERS SOMEWHERE, EACH OF WHOM APPEARS ONLY ONCE ON MY TRAVELS. CAN YOU FIND ONE OTHER CHARACTER WHO APPEARS IN EVERY SCENE? ALSO IN EVERY SCENE, CAN YOU SPOT WIZARD WHITEBEARD'S SCROLL, MY KEY, WOOF'S BONE, WENDA'S CAMERA, AND ODLAW'S BINOCULARS?

WOW! WHAT A SEARCH!

Wally

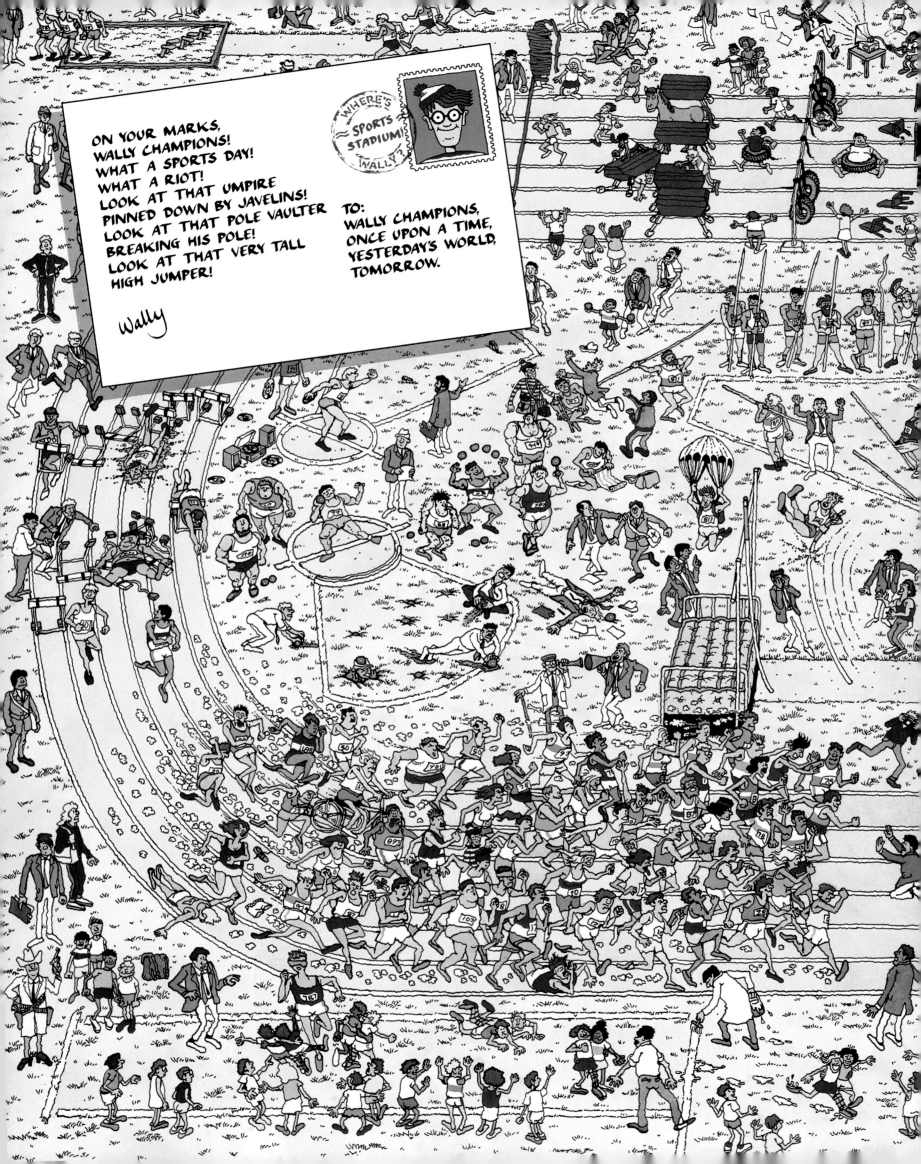

THE GREAT WHERE'S WALLY? CHECKLIST
Hundreds more things for Wally-watchers to watch out for!

IN TOWN

- A dog on a roof
- A man on a fountain
- A man about to trip over a dog's lead
- A car crash
- A keen barber
- People in a street, watching TV
- A puncture caused by a Roman arrow
- A tearful tune
- A boy attacked by a plant
- A waiter who isn't concentrating
- Two fireman waving at each other
- A face on a wall
- A man coming out of a man-hole
- A man feeding pigeons
- A bicycle crash

SKI SLOPES

- A man reading on a roof
- A flying skier
- A runaway skier
- A backward skier
- A portrait in snow
- An illegal fisherman
- A snowball in the neck
- Two unconscious skiers
- Two skiers hitting trees
- An Alpine horn
- A snow skier
- A flag collector
- Four people in yellow-hooded tops
- A skier up a tree
- A water skier on snow
- A Yeti
- A skiing reindeer
- A roof jumper
- Someone crashing through five skiers

THE RAILWAY STATION

- A man falling from a train
- A break-down on tracks
- A trolley carrying five suitcases
- People being knocked over by a door
- A man about to step on a ball
- Three different times at the same time
- A wheelbarrow pram
- A face on a train
- Five people reading one newspaper
- A struggling bag carrier
- A show-off with suitcases
- A man losing everything from his suitcases
- A smoking train
- A squeeze on a bench
- A dog tearing a man's trousers
- A man sitting on a suitcase
- A hand caught between doors
- A cattle stampede
- A man breaking a weighing machine

ON THE BEACH

- A dog wearing sunglasses like its owner's
- A man who is overdressed
- A muscular medallion man
- A popular girl
- A water skier on water
- A stripy photo
- A punctured lilo
- A donkey who likes ice-cream
- A man being squashed
- A punctured beach ball
- A human pyramid
- A human stepping-stone
- Two odd friends
- A cowboy
- A human donkey
- Age and beauty
- Two red and yellow unbrellas
- Two men with vests, one without
- A boy being tortured by a spider
- A show-off with sandcastles
- A gang of hat robbers
- A cream-coloured dog
- Three protruding tongues
- Two oddly fitting hats
- An odd couple
- Five sprinters
- A towel with a hole in it
- A punctured hovercraft
- A boy who's not allowed any ice-cream

CAMP SITE

- A bull in a hedge
- Bull horns
- A shark in a canal
- A bull seeing red
- A careless kick
- Tea in a lap
- A low bridge
- People knocked over by a mallet
- A man surprised undressing
- A bicycle tyre about to be punctured
- Five dogs
- A scarecrow that doesn't work
- A wigwam
- Large biceps
- A collapsed tent
- A smoking barbecue
- A fisherman catching old boots
- A winning penny-farthing
- A boy scout making fire
- A roller hiker
- A man blowing up a boat
- A camper's butler
- Runners on the road
- A bull chasing two people
- Scruffy campers
- Thirsty walkers

SPORTS STADIUM

- Three pairs of feet, sticking out of sand
- A cowboy starting races
- Hopeless hurdlers
- Ten children with fifteen legs
- Record discs thrown by a discus thrower
- A shot-put juggler
- An ear trumpet
- A vaulting horse
- A runner with two wheels
- A parachuting vaulter
- A Scotsman with a caber
- An elephant pulling a rope
- People being knocked over by a hammer
- A gardener
- Three frogmen
- A runner without any shorts on
- A bed
- A bandaged boy
- A runner with four legs
- A sunken jumper
- Two athletes with stripy towels
- A dog chasing a cat, chasing a mouse
- A boy squirting water

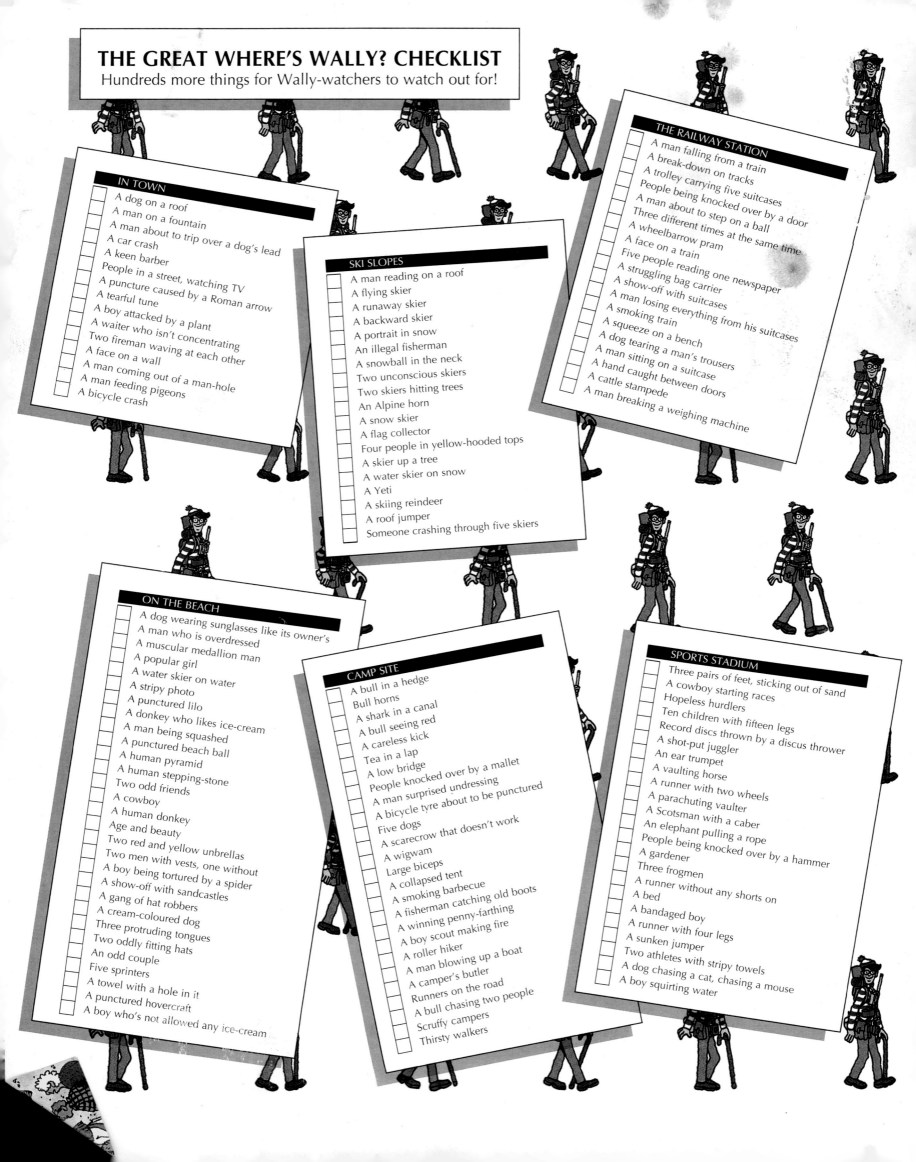

MUSEUM

- A very big skeleton
- A clown squirting water
- A boy in a catapult
- A bird's nest in a woman's hair
- A highwayman
- A popping bicep
- One circular picture frame
- A knight watching TV
- Picture robbers
- A smoking picture
- A leaking watercolour
- Fighting pictures
- A king and queen
- A rude character inside a picture
- Three cave men
- A lady wearing a red scarf
- Charioteers
- A collapsing pillar

SAFARI PARK

- Noah's Ark
- A message in a bottle
- A hippo having its teeth cleaned
- A bird's nest in an antler
- A hungry giraffe
- An ice-cream robber
- A zebra crossing
- Father Christmas
- Three owls
- A unicorn
- Caged people
- A lion next to the driver in a car
- Bears
- Tarzan
- Lion cubs
- Two ladies with red handbags
- Two queues for the toilets
- Animals' beauty parlour
- An elephant squirting water

DEPARTMENT STORE

- An ironing demonstration
- A red-suited pushchair passenger
- A man whose boots face the wrong way
- A man with heavy shopping
- A misbehaving vacuum cleaner
- Ties that match their wearers
- A man washing his clothes
- A man trying on a jacket that's too big
- A woman tripping over a ball on the floor
- A girl wearing a red anorak
- A boy riding in a trolley bag
- A glove that's alive

AT SEA

- A windsurfer
- A boat punctured by an arrow
- A sword fight with a swordfish
- A school of whales
- Seasick sailors
- A leaking diver
- A boat crash
- A bathtub
- A bearded man wearing sunglasses
- A game of noughts and crosses
- A lucky fisherman
- Three lumberjacks
- Unlucky fishermen
- Two water skiers in a tangle
- Fish robbers
- A cowboy riding a seahorse
- A fishy photo
- A man being strangled by an octopus
- Uninvited pirates climbing aboard ship
- A Chinese junk
- A wave at sea

FAIRGROUND

- A cannon at a rifle range
- A bumper car run wild
- Ten coloured hoops
- A one-armed bandit
- A ragdoll
- A runaway fairground rocket
- A runaway fairground horse
- A haunted house
- Seven lost children and a lost dog
- A tank crash
- A weightlifter dropping his weights
- Three clowns
- Three men dressed as bears

AIRPORT

- A flying saucer
- A boy sitting with the revolving luggage
- A child firing a catapult
- A leaking fuel pipe
- Flight controllers playing badminton
- A rocket
- A tower on top of the control tower
- Three watch smugglers
- Naughty children on a plane
- A forklift truck
- A wind-sock
- A chopper
- A plane that doesn't fly
- A flying Ace
- Dracula
- Five men blowing up a balloon
- Runners on a runway
- Four smoking people
- Four people falling from a plane
- A cargo of cattle
- A fire engine
- Three childish pilots
- Eighteen airport workers with yellow caps

WOW! WHAT A SEARCH!

Did you find Wally, all his friends, and all the things they lost? Did you find the one scene where Wally and Odlaw both lost their binoculars? Odlaw's binoculars are the ones nearest to him. Did you find the extra character who appears in every scene? If not, keep looking! Wow! Fantastic!

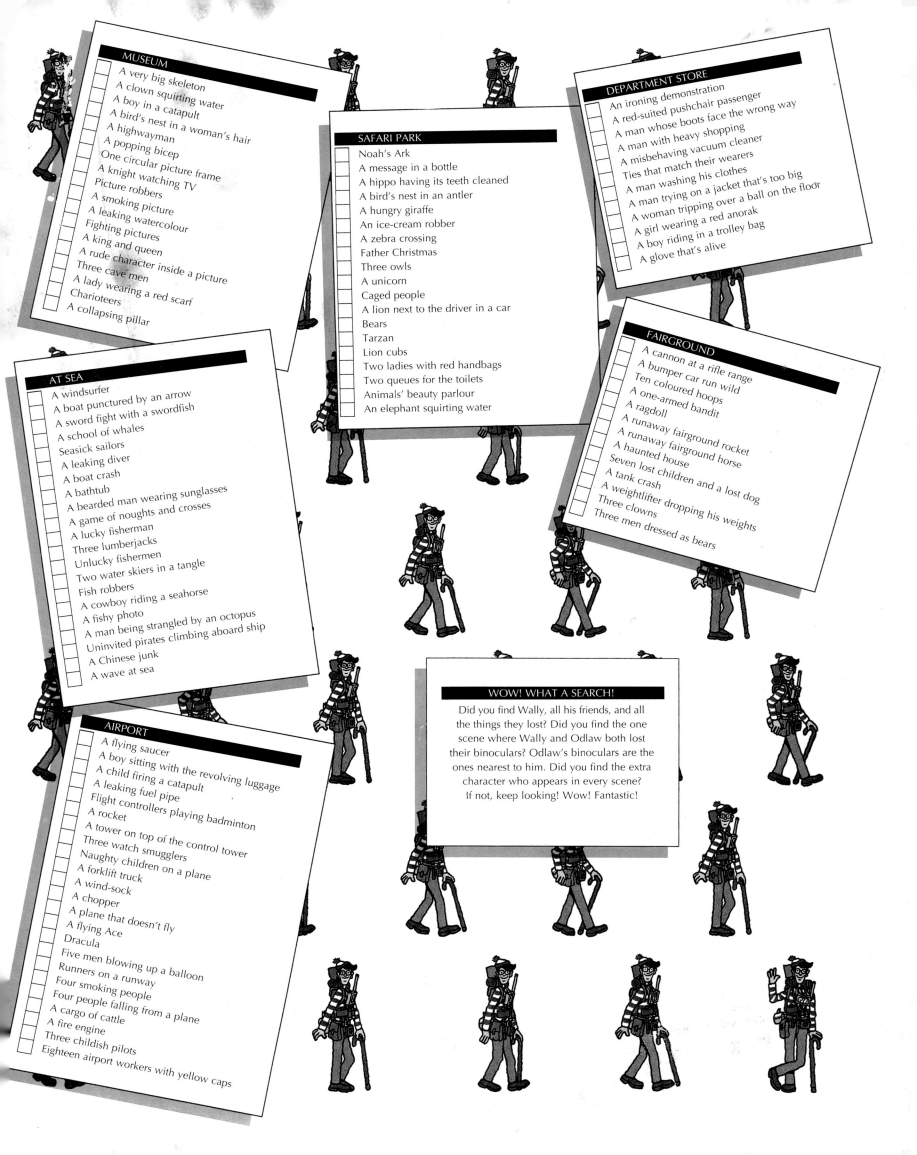